HARRISON HILL

Snap books™

BABYSITTING

Babysitting
BASICS

CARING FOR KIDS

by Leah Browning

Consultant: Beth Lapp
Certified Babysitting Training Instructor

Capstone
press®

Mankato, Minnesota

Snap Books are published by Capstone Press,
151 Good Counsel Drive, P.O. Box 669, Mankato, Minnesota 56002.
www.capstonepress.com

Library of Congress Cataloging-in-Publication Data
Browning, Leah.
    Babysitting basics: caring for kids / Leah Browning.
    p.cm.—(Snap books. Babysitting)
    Summary: "An overview for pre-teens and teens of the many aspects of babysitting"—Provided
by publisher.
    Includes bibliographical references and index.
    ISBN-13: 978-0-7368-6462-6 (hardcover)
    ISBN-10: 0-7368-6462-8 (hardcover)
    1. Babysitting—Juvenile literature. I. Title II. Series.
HQ769.5.L34 2007
649'.10248—dc22   2006001735

Editor: Becky Viaene
Designer: Jennifer Bergstrom
Photo Researcher/Photo Editor: Kelly Garvin

Photo Credits: Capstone Press/Karon Dubke, cover, 7 (game pieces), 8, 10–11, 11 (game pieces), 14–15, 20–21,
21 (pacifier), 23, 27; Corbis/Laura Dwight, 19; Corbis/Mika/zefa, 6–7; Corbis/Rob & Sas, 5; Corbis/Will & Deni McIntyre, 28;
Getty Images Inc./Stone/David Young-Wolff, 17; The Image Bank/Ross Whitaker, 25; Leah Browning/Photo taken by Greg
Becker, 32; Photodisc, 12 (popcorn); PhotoEdit Inc./David Young Wolff, 13; PhotoEdit Inc./Myrleen Ferguson Cate, 9

Table of Contents

Yeah! The Babysitter's Here

Do you love children? Are you patient and responsible? Have you ever thought about becoming a babysitter?

As most babysitters will tell you, the job isn't easy. But it does have lots of rewards. Seeing a child's face light up when you walk into a room makes you feel great. And babysitting is a fun way to earn money after school and on weekends.

You might not have experience with babysitting and aren't quite sure what to expect. Parents expect babysitters to be in charge while they're gone. This book will get you on the road to success.

TERRIFIC TRAINING
See if the American Red Cross offers a babysitting class in your area. A class can help you prepare for babysitting jobs and make you feel confident in tough situations.

Keeping Kids Safe

Sit on the floor and look around your home. Now imagine you want to touch and taste everything you see.

Babies and young children are naturally curious. They learn about their world by exploring it, often by putting everything they touch into their mouths. That's why you need to watch children at all times.

Parents are counting on you to keep their kids safe. It's your job to keep them away from anything that could hurt or choke them.

Choking Hazards

* Toys with small removable parts
* Game pieces
* Jewelry
* Buttons
* Ribbons and strings
* Balloons
* Coins
* Other small items

Safety First

The house where you're babysitting may not be as safe as it looks. Many items that may not look harmful to you are dangerous to young children. When you babysit for small children, check whether they can reach any dangerous items. Move harmful objects you find and shut doors to bathrooms and other rooms with hazards. Most importantly, never leave young children alone.

Safety also means keeping people out of the house. Keep the doors and windows locked while you're babysitting. Don't open the door for anyone.

Common Household Dangers

* Stairs
* Electrical outlets
* Appliances
* Hot or heavy pans
* Hot food or drinks
* Knives or sharp scissors
* Toilets, bathtubs, and pools
* Household chemicals

Entertaining Everyone

You probably won't get a 10-year-old to play peek-a-boo. And you shouldn't let a baby play Monopoly with his older brother.

It's a good idea to learn which activities are safe and fun for different ages.

Babies

Newborn babies need to be held and fed, not entertained. Once babies are a few months old, they will enjoy noisy, colorful toys.

Toddlers

A toddler is a young child who is learning or has just learned to walk. Kids around this age are learning how to use their bodies and brains. Toddlers enjoy building with blocks, singing, and dancing.

Older Children

Older children are interested in more complicated toys and games. With kids who are old enough to talk, you don't have to guess which activities they would like. Just ask!

Time to Eat

Children often enjoy helping make snacks and meals. Let them help measure, add ingredients, and stir.

Just remember to have everyone wash their hands before and after doing anything with food. Keep children away from knives, the stove and oven, and hot drinks or hot food.

Be smart about what foods you give to children. Ask their parents if there are any foods the children can't have. Be especially careful if the child has food allergies.

Foods that Commonly Cause Choking

* Nuts
* Hard or sticky candy
* Grapes
* Popcorn
* Hotdogs

Pay close attention to the type and size of food you give to children who are younger than four. Kids can choke if they're given foods that they aren't old enough to eat. Cut large pieces of food into small, bite-size pieces.

Tidy up after a meal or snack. Put leftovers in the refrigerator, and stack dishes neatly in the sink.

Washing Up

You're done feeding the baby. And you're not sure if more food is in his tummy or on his face.

Make sure to wash those messy fingers and that face. Leave the baby in the highchair while using a warm, wet washcloth to gently wipe him clean.

Older children may need help washing up too. You may need to get them a step stool so they can reach the sink to wash their hands. Even kids who can clean up by themselves may need to be reminded to wash.

WHAT WOULD YOU DO?

A toddler's parents asked you to give him a bath. While you're washing his hair, you hear his older sister calling for help. She was running and tripped.

SIMPLE SOLUTION

Take the toddler out of the tub and wrap him in a towel. Bring him with you, or place him in a safe place, like a crib. Then you can help his sister.

Parents usually won't ask you to give children a shower or bath, but sometimes they may. When giving a bath or shower, make sure that you have soap and other supplies within reach. Use your elbow to check the water temperature before the child gets in.

During a bath, always have at least one hand supporting the baby. Young children's heads are the heaviest parts of their bodies. If they tip over, they may not have the strength to get back up.

A child can drown quickly in a small amount of water. Never leave babies or young children alone in or around water, even for a single second. If you must leave the bathroom, always take the child with you.

It's Potty Time

It's the moment you've been dreading. The cute, cuddly baby is giving off a terrible smell. Even worse, you see a brown stain leaking out of his diaper.

Before you start changing the baby, gather your supplies, including diapers and wipes. Lay the baby on his back on top of a changing table or blanket. Take off the dirty diaper. Wipe the baby's bottom from front to back. Put a clean diaper on the baby. Place the baby in a safe place, such as a crib. Then throw the dirty diaper away and wash your hands.

Helpful Hint

You might not feel comfortable using a changing table because babies can be squirmy and roll off. You can place a blanket on the floor and change the baby there instead.

Potty Training

Children who are potty training need to go to the bathroom often. You may even need to remind them to go. Accidents are common when children are switching from diapers to the toilet. Even older children who are potty trained may have accidents.

Remember that children don't have accidents on purpose. They may be embarrassed or ashamed. Never punish or speak angrily to a child who has had an accident. Instead, be kind. Clean up the mess and help the child wash up and get into dry clothing.

If the child does make it to the bathroom in time, praise her. You will probably need to wipe for her. Wiping is a difficult skill for children to learn. Be sure to wash your hands after wiping. Encourage her to wash hands too.

WHAT WOULD YOU DO?

You are babysitting for a 5-year-old boy. Suddenly, you notice a dark spot on his pants and a puddle by his feet. He looks embarrassed and hangs his head.

SIMPLE SOLUTION

Help the boy get out of the wet clothes, wash up, and get into dry clothes. Use soap and a wet paper towel to clean the floor. Rinse the pants in a sink with soap and hang them over the tub to dry.

Curing the Crying

Babies cry because they have a problem. The tricky part is figuring out what the problem is and how to fix it.

Stay calm and look for clues. Does the baby need to be changed? Is she hungry? Does she want her pacifier? Do your best to identify and solve the problem.

Reasons Babies Cry

* Hunger
* Wet or dirty diaper
* Too hot or too cold
* Fear
* Tiredness
* Pain

Ways to Comfort a Baby

* Walking back and forth
* Rocking
* Singing
* Cuddling
* Giving the baby a pacifier

WHEN TO GET HELP

If a baby's crying is starting to make you angry, put the baby in a crib or other safe place. Go into another room for a minute and take a couple of deep breaths, or count to 10. Pick the baby up when you feel calm again. Call the baby's parents, your parents, or a responsible adult for help.

Never shake or spank a baby. Even gently shaking a baby can cause brain damage or death. If a baby has been crying for 20 to 30 minutes, it's time to get help.

Like babies, older children cry for a reason. Again, do your best to identify and solve the problem. At some point, most children experience separation anxiety. They are afraid or worried about being apart from their parents. These feelings are a normal part of growing up.

Be calm and reassuring, then gently distract upset children with a toy or a game. Try to comfort children who are scared or sad. Reassure them that their parents will return, but tell the truth. Don't say, "They'll be right back," if they're not expected until 2 a.m.

Reasons Older Children Cry

* Hunger
* Frustration or anger
* Fear
* Sadness
* Tiredness
* Pain

Even though you're a careful babysitter, children may still get hurt while you're watching them. Clean and bandage a scrape. Apply ice to a little bump. If there is a serious injury, call 911 or the child's parents for help.

WHEN TO CALL 911

You should call 911 for serious injuries, such as:

* Bleeding that won't stop
* Choking that stops breathing
* Loss of consciousness

Misbehavior

Babysitting can be lots of fun, as long as everyone is getting along. But do you know what to do if kids start fighting?

Brothers and sisters may fight over many things, including your attention. Help them calm down so they don't hurt each other. Occasionally kids will fight with you. "But Mom lets me!" is a common complaint. Your job is to calmly and firmly enforce the rules. It may be hard to stay calm, especially when children throw tantrums.

Children have tantrums when they are tired, hungry, or frustrated. During a tantrum they may scream, sob, kick, or roll on the floor. It may seem easier to give children what they want. Still, you need to stay calm during a tantrum. Giving in only teaches children that they can get what they want by screaming.

Helpful Hint

No matter how horribly a child is behaving, try to stay calm. If you can't control the situation, get help. Call the child's parents, your parents, or a responsible adult.

Putting Kids to Bed

When it's close to bedtime, children almost never immediately brush their teeth, put on their pajamas, and go to bed.

Most of the time, you should expect some resistance at bedtime. To make preparing for bed easier, slow things down. Do a puzzle or read a book together, which quiets the activity level.

Give older children some notice. Let them know when there are 10 minutes until bedtime. After children go to sleep, stay awake and nearby. Make sure you are close enough to hear if a child is crying or having trouble breathing. Quietly check on babies and young children every 20 to 30 minutes.

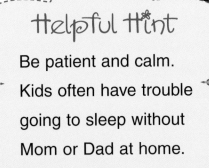

Helpful Hint

Be patient and calm. Kids often have trouble going to sleep without Mom or Dad at home.

27

A Job Well Done!

Babysitting is an adventure. It can make you feel like a celebrity, a clown, or a zookeeper—sometimes all on the same night. But with the right preparation and patience, you can be ready for just about anything. So plan ahead, do your best, and enjoy the ride!

Checklist:

Things you should know before the parents leave

Make sure that you have all the instructions you will need. Get a tour of the home, ask questions, and write down the following information:

✓ At least one phone number where the parents can be reached, such as a cell phone

✓ Address and phone number of the home you are in

✓ If your parents are not nearby, the address and phone number of a responsible adult that the family knows well

✓ Time parents expect to be home

✓ Emergency numbers

✓ Location of items in the home such as first aid supplies and exits

✓ Where to find clean diapers and clothes

✓ Ideas to soothe the baby, such as offering a pacifier, being rocked, or being sung to

✓ Bedtime rituals for the children, including time to go to bed and whether they like to be sung to or read to

✓ Whether the child has homework, chores, or other responsibilities

✓ Any other rules that you should know regarding the home, food, or misbehavior

Glossary

allergy (ALL-ur-jee)—an extremely high sensitivity to something in the environment such as dust, pollen, perfume, certain foods, or animals

choking hazard (CHO-king HA-zurd)—an item that is dangerous because it can cause someone to stop or almost stop breathing

pacifier (PA-sih-fie-er)—a rubber or plastic nipple for a baby to suck on

potty training (PAH-tee TRAYN-ing)—learning to use the toilet

separation anxiety (sep-uh-RAY-shun ang-ZI-ih-tee)—fear or worry about being apart from someone

tantrum (TAN-truhm)—a fit of bad temper

Quick Tips

* If an item is small enough to fit through a toilet paper tube, babies and toddlers could choke on it.

* If you need to go to the bathroom, put babies or little children in a safe place, such as a crib.

* Ask about entertainment. Find out if the children are allowed to watch television, play video games, or use the computer, and for how long.

* When you agree to babysit, ask the children's parents how old the children are and what they like to do. Then you can think of a few activities ahead of time.

Read More

Brown, Harriet. *The Babysitter's Handbook: The Care and Keeping of Kids.* Middleton, Wis.: Pleasant Company, 1999.

Greene, Caroline. *The Babysitter's Handbook.* New York: DK, 1995.

Kuch, K.D. *The Babysitter's Handbook.* KidBacks. New York: Random House, 1997.

Murkoff, Heidi Eisenberg. *The What to Expect Baby-sitter's Handbook.* New York: Workman, 2003.

Internet Sites

FactHound offers a safe, fun way to find Internet sites related to this book. All of the sites on FactHound have been researched by our staff.

Here's how:

1. Visit *www.facthound.com*

2. Choose your grade level.

3. Type in this book ID **0736864628** for age-appropriate sites. You may also browse subjects by clicking on letters, or by clicking on pictures and words.

4. Click on the **Fetch It** button.

Facthound will fetch the best sites for you!

About the Author

Leah Browning has always loved babies and children. In fact, as a child, she wanted to have 12 children of her own. She grew up in New Mexico, where she began babysitting at the age of 12.

Now an adult, Leah is a stay-at-home mother and writer. Her articles, essays, stories, and poems have appeared in a variety of publications including *Mothering Magazine*, *Tucson Parent Magazine*, and *Chicken Soup for the Preteen Soul 2*.

Index